CUT and CARVE
CANDLES

CUT and CARVE CANDLES

BEAUTIFUL CANDLES TO
DIP, CARVE, TWIST & CURL

By Dana Marie Brooks

EDITOR: Joanne O'Sullivan

SENIOR EDITOR: Paige Gilchrist

ART DIRECTOR: Stacey Budge

DESIGNER: Eric Stevens

PHOTOGRAPHER: Evan Bracken
(how-to photography), John Widman
(project photography)

COVER DESIGNER: Barbara Zaretsky

ASSOCIATE ART DIRECTOR: Shannon Yokeley

EDITORIAL ASSISTANCE: Delores Gosnell,
Rosemary Kast, Jeff Hamilton

Library of Congress Cataloging-in-Publication Data

Brooks, Dana Marie.
 Cut and carve candles : beautiful candles to dip, carve, twist & curl / by
Dana Brooks.-- 1st ed.
    p. cm.
 Includes index.
 ISBN 1-57990-462-9 (hard cover)
 1. Candlemaking. I. Title.
TT896.5.B76 2004
745.593'32--dc22

                                        2004004989

10 9 8 7 6 5 4 3 2 1

First Edition

Published by Lark Books, A Division of
Sterling Publishing Co., Inc.
387 Park Avenue South, New York, N.Y. 10016

© 2004, Dana Brooks

Distributed in Canada by Sterling Publishing,
c/o Canadian Manda Group, One Atlantic Ave., Suite 105
Toronto, Ontario, Canada M6K 3E7

Distributed in the U.K. by Guild of Master Craftsman Publications Ltd., Castle Place,
166 High Street, Lewes, East Sussex, England
BN7 1XU
Tel: (+ 44) 1273 477374, Fax: (+ 44) 1273 478606, Email: pubs@thegmcgroup.com,
Web: www.gmcpublications.com

Distributed in Australia by Capricorn Link (Australia) Pty Ltd.,
P.O. Box 704, Windsor, NSW 2756 Australia

If you have questions or comments about this book, please contact:
Lark Books
67 Broadway
Asheville, NC 28801
(828) 253-0467

Manufactured in China

ISBN 1-57990-462-9

Contents

Introduction

Looking at the beautiful twists and swirls of cut and carve candles, you may be convinced that making them is a complicated, technical process. Like soft waves of glossy icing or delicate ribbons of sugary candy, cut and carve candles have a look that never fails to capture your attention. But learning the art of candle carving is well within your reach if you've got just a little time and patience to invest. It won't take long before your efforts pay off and you're creating these extraordinary candles yourself.

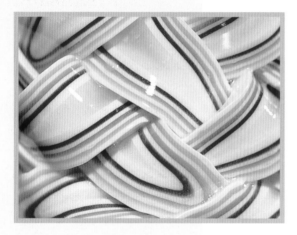

The secret to the fanciful designs you see is a dipping process that adds layers and layers of colored wax to a core candle that can be made or purchased. Cutting into the dipped candle reveals the kaleidoscope of colors created by these repeated dips in wax. When you pull, twist, curl, and shape the strips of wax you've cut, you create a sculpture in wax that glows from within, casting captivating shadows and spreading a soft, warm light to fill your room or brighten up your outdoor space.

The Getting Started section of the book will guide you through the process of creating cut and carve candles, from purchasing the right materials, to setting up your work area, preparing wax, dipping, carving, and finishing your candles. You won't need a lot of expensive equipment to get started—in fact, you probably have some of what you'll need in your kitchen already. You'll learn how to make a core candle—the base of a cut and carve candle (making your own will save you money). Step-by-step photos show you the basic cuts, such as scrolls, loops, and twists. You can try your hand at making your first candle by following the instructions for the sample project, a scroll candle. The easy-to-follow photos illustrate the techniques from start to finish. When your candle is not turning out quite the way you had hoped, turn to the Troubleshooting section for advice on how to solve common problems in the candlemaking process.

In the Projects section of the book, you'll find 20 different demonstration candles to make, each of which combines different techniques for unique designs. From a simple column candle with rows of twists, to an elaborate basket weave candle with overlapping ribbons of wax, each candle project helps build your technical and design skills. Once you've mastered the basics, you can go on to create specialty and novelty candles that make wonderful gifts for weddings and other special occasions. You'll be surprised by the wide variety of effects you can achieve by combining the basic cuts with some new techniques and a few embellishments.

When I first began making candles almost eight years ago, I found numerous books on candlemaking, but none specifically tailored to making the elaborate carved candles that I had always admired. Through trial, error, and experimentation, I learned the craft first as a hobby, creating gifts for holidays and special occasions. Now candle carving is a business that I love. I'm excited to share with you my passion for and knowledge of making cut and carve candles through this book, so that you can start creating your own masterpieces with confidence.

GETTING STARTED

Despite their impressive appearance, cut and carve candles are easy to make once you've learned the basic techniques and gotten some trial-and-error experience. You don't need to be an experienced candlemaker to create them—just have a willingness to learn and a little patience. You also don't need to invest a lot in supplies or materials to get started. You can find many of the things you need in your kitchen or garage and can easily find the rest through candlemaking suppliers or at your local craft store. Here's a list to get you started.

Equipment, Materials, and Tools

Double-boiler system. Since paraffin wax can't be heated over direct heat (it can get hot enough to ignite), you'll need a double-boiler system to melt it. Basically, a double boiler system consists of a container that holds your wax and a pot in which the wax-holding container sits. You can set up the double-boiler system on top of your stove

Container for wax

or use hot plates if you'll be making your candles in a location outside your kitchen. You'll need one burner for each color of wax you use, so even if you do use your kitchen, you may need hot plates for additional colors of wax. Hot plates can be purchased at discount stores and are fairly inexpensive.

Container for wax. You'll need a stainless-steel container for melting the wax in your double boiler. You can use empty coffee tins, but they will begin to corrode over time. For long-term use, it's better to use containers made specifically for candlemaking. You can purchase the containers from on-line candlemaking suppliers or craft stores.

Dipping vat. This method is easier than the double-boiler system, but it is more expensive and generally not practical for the first-time home candlemaker. The dipping vat uses the same concept as the double-boiler system, but combines several colors into one system and has a temperature gauge to keep the wax at a constant temperature. This will become a necessary instrument if you begin to make several candles at once and prefer to switch colors on a regular basis.

Kitchen or candy thermometer. You can find these at grocery, kitchen supply, or craft stores. Candle-supply companies also sell thermometers, but they will usually be a little more expensive.

Drop cloth and wax paper (optional but recommended). To protect the walls and floor where you'll be working, make sure you cover nearby surfaces, such as the floor and walls, with a drop cloth. The tabletop can be covered with wax paper.

Double-boiler system

Paraffin wax. Most companies distinguish different types of paraffin wax by their melting points and intended use. (The melting point is the point at which, when heated, the wax will liquefy. For example, 3035 means the wax will melt between 130 to 135°F [54 and 57°C].) For the purposes of making core candles used for carving (see page 12), use wax with a melting point around 135°F (57°C). If a supplier does not give the melting point, choose the wax designed for carving candles. Finding the right wax combination takes a little trial and error. I use a 50/50 mixture of 2530 and 4045. You can also use a wax that is specially formulated for candle carving.

Wax generally comes in 10 to 11-lb. (4.5 to 4.9 kg) slabs or in a 50 to 55-lb. (22.5 to 25.9 kg) box. Most craft stores will only sell it by the slab, which is usually more expensive than buying by the bulk (the 50 to 55-lb. [22.7 to 25 kg] box). Most on-line candle-supply companies sell the wax by the box—the more you buy, the less you pay per pound.

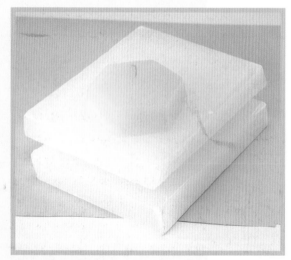

Wax blocks and slabs

Wax color pigment, white pigment dye, or white titanium oil paint. Do NOT use regular candle dye for cut and carve candles. Pigments give you a richer color and help prevent the colors from bleeding. They are available at most on-line candle-supply companies. Pigments tend to be a little more expensive than regular candle dye, but they're perfect for cut and carve candles.

Pigment dyes and color fade inhibitor

White pigment dye or oil paint is used to color the wax for the white layers between the colors. To use the oil paint, just squeeze it into the wax and stir. You can find titanium white oil paint at fine art or craft supply stores, or on-line art-supply companies (which usually sell it for less).

Color fade inhibitor (optional). This product helps prevent fading due to sun and certain lighting. You can find it at most candlemaking supply sources.

Core candles. All cut and carve candles consist of a core candle and several layers of wax. You can make your own (see page 12), or you can find websites that sell cores specifically for the purpose of cut and carve candles.

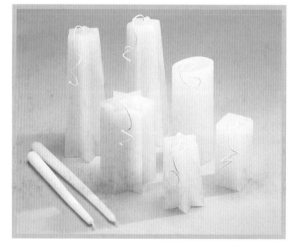

Core candles and tapers

Tea light or oil lamp (optional). Rather than burn down your core candle, you may choose to insert a tea light or oil lamp (a small glass or plastic container that is filled with oil and placed inside the candle) into your completed candle. For instructions on creating a cavity for holding a tea light or oil lamp, see page 24.

S hook or meat hook. Tie the core candle to this hook for dipping and carving. It can be purchased at most hardware stores.

Bucket of water (cool water bath). Use a bucket of water that is tall enough and wide enough to dip the entire candle. Plastic trashcans work great and can be purchased at just about any store.

Molds. Molds come in different heights and shapes. There are star-shaped molds, ovals, squares, and ball molds. The best mold to start out with for carving purposes is the 6-point-star metal candle mold. Candle molds can be purchased at most craft-supply stores as well as from on-line sources. Generally speaking, you can find a better deal on molds at on-line candlemaking-supply companies.

Oval and six-point-star molds

Wicks. Use braided cotton wicks, one size below what is generally used for the size candle you are pouring. For example, a 3-inch-wide (7.6 cm) candle would normally use a 1/0 size wick, but for cut and carve candles, you would use a 3/0 wick. Most companies will give the recommended use for each wick they supply. Wicks can be purchased at most craft-supply stores or on-line candle-supply companies and are fairly inexpensive.

Small screw or plug. These are used to plug the end of the mold where the wick comes through. They are a must and are very inexpensive. They can be purchased at most craft stores and on-line craft-supply companies. If you choose to use screws, you can purchase them at any hardware store, too.

Mold sealer. This is a putty-type material that is placed over the screw and wick to prevent the wax from seeping out the bottom of the mold. It comes in two colors—white and gray. I have found that the white mold sealer works better. The gray

seems to be more tacky and messy. Mold sealer is inexpensive and can be purchased at most craft stores or on-line candle-supply companies.

Wick rod. This is used to tie the wick and hold it centered while the wax is cooling. Actual wick rods can be purchased at on-line candle-supply companies and are very inexpensive.

Scissors. You'll need these to cut the wick from the wick rod.

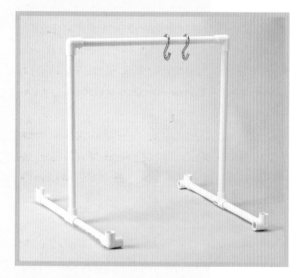

Carving station. You will need an area for the candle to hang freely for carving after it has been dipped. The candle needs to be at eye level, so decide whether you will do your carving while standing or sitting. You can make a tabletop carving station, like the one shown in the picture, by simply screwing together a few lengths of PVC piping with PVC pipe elbows. You'll need the piping to be narrow enough for the S hook to slip on and off easily. You can basically set up a carving station anywhere that you can hang a candle. Just keep in mind that if you're making several candles, it will take time, so you'll want to be in a comfortable position.

Left to right: Spade bit for drilling holes for oil lamps and tea lights, ribbon-carving tool, paring knife, copper tubing

Paring knife. This is your basic carving tool. It must have a sharp edge to make clean cuts in the wax. You can find this kind of knife at kitchen stores or grocery stores, and they're fairly inexpensive.

Ribbon-carving tool/potter's tool. This tool is used to make the spiral twists on the candle. It can be purchased at most craft stores or at on-line craft-supply stores. Make sure that the cutting side is sharp before you use it. A dull blade will make jagged cuts.

Paper towels. You'll need paper towels to clean up your carving knife before each carving. They're also handy to have around in case of minor spills.

Copper tubing, $3/4$ to $1 1/2$-inch (1.9 to 3.8 cm) (or similar tool). Copper tubing is used to trim the top of the candle (around the wick) for a clean look and burn. Other items, like an apple corer, can be used, depending on how large you want the hole. Copper tubing can be purchased at most hardware or plumbing-supply stores.

Drill and spade bit. To create a cavity for holding a tea light or oil lamp, you will need a drill and spade bit to remove the wax from your completed candle (see page 24 for instructions).

Candle glaze. This is used for the finishing touch on the cut and carve candles. It protects the candle and gives it a shiny, glossy look. Candle glaze is a little more expensive than the other supplies; however, it will last through many candles. Glaze really brings out the beauty of the candle and takes away a lot of the little imperfections. It can be purchased at most on-line candle-supply companies.

LITTLE EXTRAS

The following items are not necessary, but might be helpful to have around.

Embellishments. Add small seashells, starfish, decals, and other embellishments to candles as needed. Embellishments are usually added to the candle after you are finished carving your design. They can be embedded into the wax or attached to the wax with pins. They are also dipped into the clear wax for the final dip and then into the glaze to secure the items in place.

Mold release. To help in the process of removing the candle from the mold, you can use a professional mold release, or a household spray lubricant. Mold release is available at most craft-supply stores or on-line candle-supply companies.

Wax remover. This product cleans wax from candle molds and also helps aid in the release of candles from the mold. It can be purchased at most craft supply stores or on-line candle supply companies.

Needle-nose pliers. These will come in handy if you need to pick up the finished candle before it is actually dry. You can also use them if needed to help pull a candle from the mold. They can be purchased at most hardware stores.

Measuring cup or ladle. If your wax container is too big to pick up and pour by hand, you will need a cup or ladle for pouring the melted wax into the mold.

Making a Core Candle

You can purchase premade core candles from a candlemaking supplier, or you can make your own. Purchasing premade candle cores saves you time, but if you do plan on making a lot of cut and carve candles, you may save money in the long run by investing in a few molds and making the core candles yourself. If you do decide on this option, the following instructions will guide you through the process. Once you've got a core candle, you're ready to start the dipping and carving process.

YOU WILL NEED

Metal candle mold of your choice*

Mold release spray (such as a spray-on oil lubricant)

Wick*

Wick rod*

Small screw or plug

Mold sealer

Scissors

Double-boiler system

Wax container

Paraffin wax

Candy thermometer*

Ladle or cup (optional)

*Available through candlemaking supply sources or craft stores

1 Prepare the candle mold by spraying it with a few squirts of mold release. Thread the wick through the hole in the bottom of the mold.

2 Pull the wick up to the top of the mold, and tie it to a wick rod.

3 Pull the wick snug, and insert a screw or plug into the other end to secure the wick. Be sure there is not a lot of slack in the wick.

4 Firmly press the mold sealer around the wick and screw to give it a good "seal." Cut the wick. IMPORTANT: Since the bottom of the mold is actually the top of the candle, be sure to leave enough wick (approximately 6 to 8 inches [15.2 to 20.3 cm]) to tie to a hook for carving.

5 Put your wax container inside the outer pot, and fill the outer pot with water, about halfway up. Position the wax in the wax container and heat it until it reaches about 155 to 160°F (68 to 71°C).

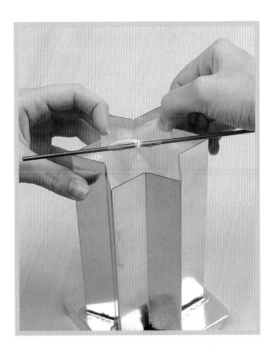

6 On a level surface, slowly pour the wax into the mold. If the wax container is too large or heavy, use a cup or ladle to transfer the wax. As the candle cools, you will notice an indentation forming on top of the wax. Use a needle or wick rod to poke a couple of holes around the wick to let the air out. You will need to top off the candle with a little more wax as it cools.

7 Once the candle has completely cooled, remove the mold sealer and screw. Pull the sides of the mold away from the candle to loosen the grip, and remove the candle from the mold.

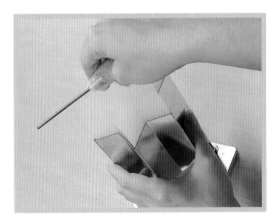

Tip: If the candle is difficult to remove, put it in the freezer for approximately 30 minutes. This causes the candle to contract, making it easy to pull out of the mold.
Tip: *Be careful not to leave the candle in the freezer for an extended period of time or it will crack.*

Candle Carving Basics

Now that you've got your core candle, you can move on to the next step in the process: dipping and carving the candle. The surface of the core candle is built up by dipping it repeatedly in different colors of wax. Once you've created as many as 20 to 30 layers of wax on top of the core candle (which make the candle as much as 1 inch [2.5 cm] thicker than when you began), you're ready to start carving. The following section will guide you through the procedure.

Preparing Your Work Area

Your work area is a very important part of candle carving. You'll need to have everything set up and ready before you begin the dipping and carving process. Be sure to cover your work area with plastic to avoid drips and splashes of wax on your walls, table, or carpet. When preparing your carving station, make sure that you have a secure, sturdy place to hang the candle and that it will hang freely at eye level. You will need a smooth surface table nearby for leveling out the candle, holding your supplies, and heating the wax. Next to the area, you will need a large bucket of water for the dipping process. A 10-gallon trashcan is appropriate. Covering your work area with wax paper will make cleaning up a breeze. It will also help keep your table smooth.

Preparing the Wax

Set up your double-boiler system with a large pot and wax container, a hot plate (or stove), water, and wax. The inner container holds the wax. This container needs to be wide enough to dip the candle and deep enough to accommodate the length of the core candle. There are cans specifically made for this purpose or you can use any stainless-steel can or a large coffee container, etc. The outer container needs to be large enough to hold the inner container

(1 to 2 inches [[2.5 to 5.2 cm] around the sides) and deep enough to hold water about one-third the way up the inner container (without overflowing when boiling). You can use any medium-to-large cooking pot for this.

Decide how many colors of wax you'll need for the candle. You will need a container of white wax and a container of clear wax for each candle you make, in addition to one container for each additional color that you choose.

Fill the inner container with wax, to about 2 inches (5.2 cm) from the top. Fill the outer container with water. Use a kitchen thermometer to melt the wax to the correct temperature of about 155 to 160°F (68 to 71°C). Note: If you have too much wax in the container, it will overflow into the water. This is not a big issue when it happens, as long as the wax doesn't land on the heat source. Just keep dipping your candle and clean the wax out of the water later.

Add the pigment dye to each container (except the clear) and let it melt (see photo, top left column, page 15). The amount of pigment dye that you will use for each color will depend on how dark you want the color. Add a little at a time until you reach the desired color. **Hint:** *the color that you see is not the actual color. To test the wax to see what the actual color will be, use an old taper candle (or something similar)*

and dip it into the wax a few times. Let the taper cool completely and that is your actual color. Be sure to stir the wax thoroughly to mix the pigment because pigment dyes tend to settle to the bottom. The white wax should be very rich in color. One to two dips should cover the previous color.

Dipping Process

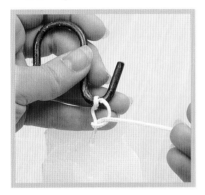

Once your wax has reached the correct temperature, tie the wick of your core candle to an S hook.

Holding onto the hook, dip the candle in your first color of wax for about 45 seconds.

After each dip, you'll need to dip the candle in the cool water bath.

Dip the candle in additional colors of wax, in the design of your choice.

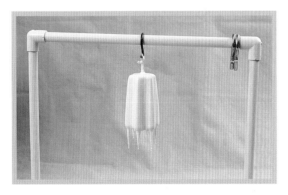

When you've got all the layers you want, hang the candle from the hook on your carving station to prepare to carve it.

Candle Carving Instructions

The actual process of carving the candle is done while the wax is warm and malleable. You are limited to a time frame of about 10 minutes once you are finished with the dipping process (described on page 15). For this reason, it's important that you work on the candle from start to finish with no interruptions. Be sure to design the candle in your head before you begin.

BASIC CUTS

As you'll notice, many of the candles projecrs in the book have the same cuts, just in different locations and patterns on the candle. Below are some of the basic cuts that you will see demonstrated. There are also many variations of the cuts shown below. Once you've got the technique down for a certain cut, try combining that cut with another on a candle. You can continue adding combinations of cuts to make up your own designs, or even make up your own unique variations on the basic cuts as you become more comfortable with carving.

Lyre Cut

Holding the knife at about a 75° angle, make a 1 to 2-inch-long (2.5 to 5 cm) cut in the candle.

Fold over the strip of wax, and attach its tip to the candle just under the bottom of the cut. Bow the wax strip slightly with your finger before reattaching it, as shown in the photo.

Basic Twist

Make a cut of desired length. Pull the wax strip away from the candle, twist it, then reattach it to the candle at the top of the cut.

Roll Cut

The roll cut is similar to the lyre cut. Make a 1 to 2-inch-long (2.5 to 5 cm) cut on your candle. Instead of folding it over, gently roll it down as if rolling it around a pencil. When you create rows of roll cuts, you achieve an elaborate effect.

Gouge

This cut is done using the ribbon tool. Position the tool in the center groove between two points on the candle. Press the tool firmly into the candle, piercing through most of the

dipped layers. Slide the tool down the candle. When you reach the desired length, gently slide the tool off of the wax strip and fold it over.

Gouge Twist

Use the ribbon tool in the same manner as for the gouge cut: press it into the groove between two points on the candle. Instead of folding the cut strip down, give the strip a few twists (to form the peppermint stick look), and then stick it back in place at the top of the cut.

Bow

There are two main variations on the bow cut.

Simple Bow

Make a 1 to 2-inch-long (2.5 to 5.2 cm) cut on two star points of the candle. Fold the wax strip created by each cut into the groove between the two points so that they meet in the center. Using your ribbon tool, make a gouge in the groove just above the point where the strips meet. Bend the wax strip over the point where the strips meet.

Bow with a Twist

Begin by making a cut near the bottom of two star points of the candle. For this candle we made the cuts above two lyre cuts, but that's a design choice that's optional. Fold each one over to the center groove between them until their tips meet in the middle. Make two more cuts above the first two, and fold the strips of wax to the center groove to meet the previous cuts.

Using the ribbon tool, make a gouge about ¹/₂ to 1 inch (1.3 to 2.5 cm) above the point where the strips meet.

Twist the wax strip and curl it around, forming a knot.

Advanced Techniques

Basket Weave

Begin by making 1 to 2-inch (2.5 to 5 cm) cuts on all six points of the candle. Fold each cut in the same direction, placing each tip where the one next to it began.

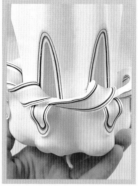

Next, make six more cuts all the way around and fold those strips in the opposite direction. This time, tuck the tips behind the first layer.

Continue this process of layering in opposite directions until you reach the desired number of rows.

Upward Cut Lyre

Upward cuts tend to be more difficult for most people. The first step is to make a small roll cut. Next, approximately 2 inches (5 cm) below the bottom of the roll, make an upward cut to the bottom of the roll. The hard part with upward cuts is to get the right depth and angle. This comes with practice.

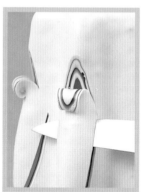

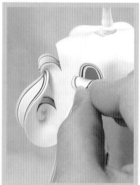

After making the upward cut, stretch the wax strip up over the small roll about 1 inch (2.5 cm). Finally, above the top of the upward cut strip, do another lyre cut.

Scroll Candle Sample Project

For your first project, try making a scroll candle, composed of several rows of roll cuts and a few gouge twists. This design is great for helping you to practice making cuts of the correct length and depth so that you can get used to the feel of the wax.

You Will Need

Double-boiler system for 2 containers of wax

4-inch tall (10.2 cm) 6-point-star core candle

S hook

Clear wax

White pigment

Bucket of cool water

Carving station

Paring knife

Ribbon-carving tool

Wax paper

Candle glaze

Scissors

Copper tubing

Preparing the Wax

Prepare the wax as described on page 14. Set up your double boilers to accommodate the clear and white wax. Stir the white pigment dye thoroughly.

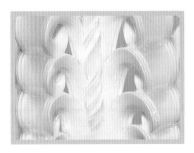

DIPPING PROCESS

1 Tie a 4-inch (10.2 cm) core candle to your S hook to begin the dipping process.

2 Dip the candle in the white wax and hold for approximately 45 seconds. For this practice candle, you'll use only white and clear wax. When you start using colors, the first dip will be your base color.

Remove the candle, let the excess wax drip off, and then dip the candle in a bucket of cool water. Remove the candle promptly, and blow or gently wipe off any water bubbles. At the beginning stages of the dipping process, it is not too important to remove all of the bubbles. After the initial dip into the wax and water, continue making swift dips from white wax to water. Do this for 5 dips of white.

Next, dip the candle in the clear wax, then water for five dips of clear wax. Continue this process for five more dips of white, then four more dips of clear and finish with five dips of white. At the end of the dipping process, you should have about 20 to 30 dips of wax. While you're making the last two to three dips, be sure to get the water bubbles off so the outside of the candle has a smooth surface. The thickness of each layer of color will depend on how many dips you make. Three dips will make a thin layer, five dips a medium layer, and so on.

CARVING PROCESS

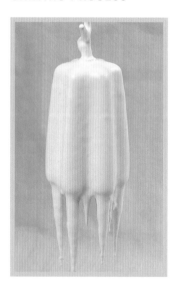

3 Hang the candle so you are looking at it at eye level. There will be long drips of wax hanging from the bottom of the candle.

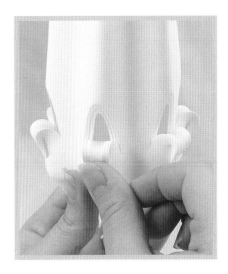

4 Gather the drippings on the bottom of the candle together so that you have a handle to hold onto while carving. **Note:** *Depending on the depth of your dipping container and the height of the candle, you may not always have enough drippings to hold on to. Gently hold the base of the candle instead, using caution not to grip too tightly.*

6 Fold over each of the cuts. Secure the tip of the wax strip to the bottom of the candle by pressing gently with your fingers, forming a lyre cut.

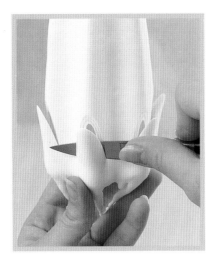

5 Holding your knife at a 75° angle, make a straight cut about 2 inches (5 cm) from the bottom of the candle. Be careful not to make the cut too deep or too thin; the thickness of the cut should be about 3/16 inch (5 mm) deep. Continue to make an identical cut in the same position of each point on the candle.

7 After the first cuts have been folded over, make another cut about 1/2 to 3/4 inch (1.3 to 1.9 cm) above the first one. Again, repeat the cut on each point of the candle in the same position.

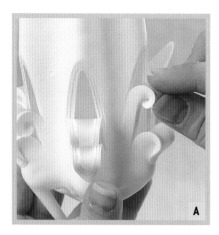

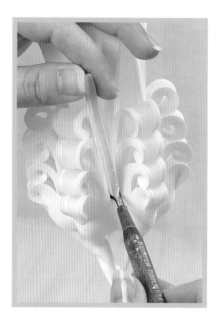

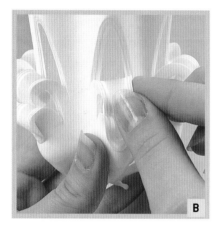

8 Roll each cut down as if rolling it around a pencil.

10 After all the rolls are finished, use the ribbon tool to make a gouge in the groove between two points of the candle. Press the sharp side of the tool into the groove, then drag it down the groove, removing a piece of wax as you go.

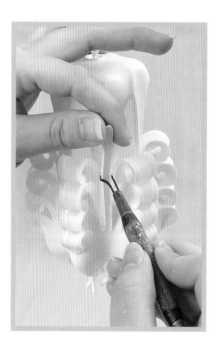

9 Continue making cuts ½ to ¾ inch (1.3 to 1.9 cm) above the previous cut until you have four rows of cuts.

11 Remove the tool from the strip of wax by loosening it and gently sliding it up the strip.

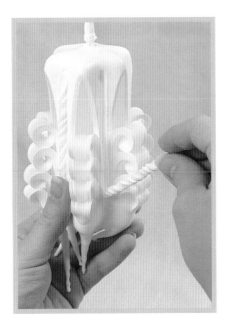

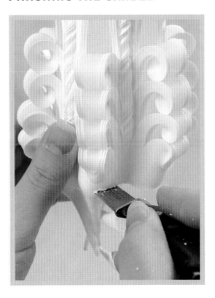

Finishing the Candle

12 Pull the strip from the candle (making sure not to pull it off at the bottom), and twist it several times.**Tip:** *If the strip does come off, simply twist it several times and reattach it to the bottom of the cut.*

14 Make sure that none of the strips have come loose from the candle. Cut the excess drippings from the bottom of the candle. Be sure to keep your knife level for a clean, even cut.

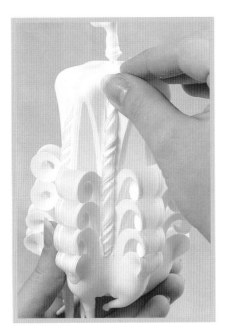

13 Reattach the strip to the candle at the top of the cut, placing the twisted strip back into the gouge.

15 Level the bottom of the candle by placing it on a flat surface and pressing firmly with the palm of your hand all the way around, until the candle sits on the flat surface without tilting.

16 After the candle is level, you will need to do a final dip in the clear wax. Don't touch the candle after the final dip — oils from your hands will get on the candle and the oil will prevent the glaze from sticking to the candle. Do NOT dip the candle into the water bucket at this point.

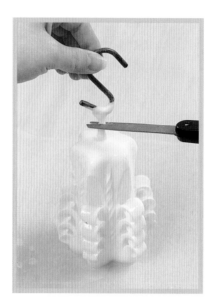

18 After about 1 to 2 minutes (or until the glaze stops dripping), set the candle on a flat surface protected with wax paper, and cut the wick from the S hook.

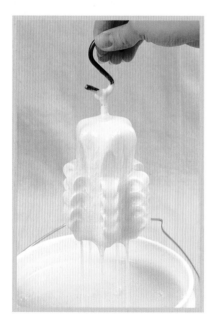

17 Dip the candle in the glaze and hang to let the excess glaze drip off. Blow off any air bubbles.

19 Use a piece of 3/4 to 1 1/2-inch (1.9 to 3.8 cm) copper tubing (or something similar), and center it around the wick. Press firmly through the wax and twist a couple times. When pressing down, be sure to press evenly on all sides. Remove the tubing and then remove the wax from the hole. You are removing the dipped layers of wax to reveal the core candle.

Note: *The size of the copper tubing used will depend on your intended use for the candle. If you are making an oil lamp (see below), use 3/4-inch (1.7 cm) tubing. If you are making a hole for the tea light (see below), use 1 1/2-inch (3.8 cm) tubing. If you won't be inserting anything into the candle, 1-inch (2.5 cm) tubing will work.*

candle after using the copper tubing around the wick. Once the candle is dry to the touch, use a spade bit and handheld drill to create a hole in the candle. Center the bit over the opening you created with the tubing. Hold the drill straight over the candle and slowly drill the wax out until you reach the desired depth. When you are done drilling, blow off any wax shavings and insert your oil lamp or tea light.

Congratulations! You have completed your first cut and carve candle! If the candle is not level after it is completely dried and cooled, it can be leveled off using a hot plate (see page 29).

ALTERNATIVE

If you'd like your candle to last longer, you can insert an oil lamp or tea light into the top of the candle instead of burning the core candle. To adjust the candle to accommodate the tea light or oil lamp, you need to drill a hole at the top of the

WHAT TO DO WITH LEFTOVER WAX

MUSHROOM CANDLE

Make a mushroom candle with the leftover wax you cut off the dipped candle.

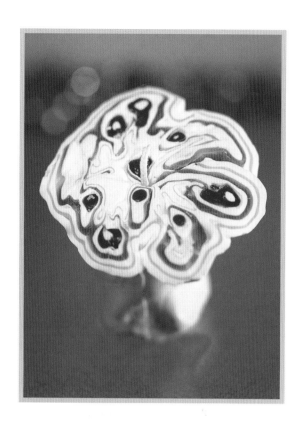

1 While it's still warm and malleable, grab the wax dripping "handle" with one hand under the "head." Use your paring knife to cut off the handle. Flatten the head with your hand to form the mushroom's stem.

2 Cut the tip off the bottom.

3 Place the mushroom on the table, and squeeze to form a base so that it will stand on its own.

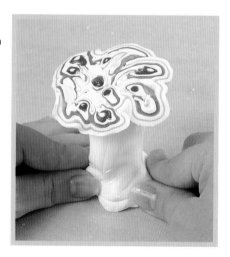

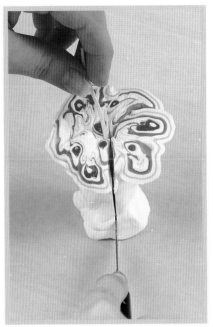

4 To insert the wick, place the wick in the center of the candle. Dip your knife into the hot water, and immediately put the knife on top of the wick in the center of the mushroom and cut all the way to the bottom (don't worry about wiping the knife after dipping in the hot water). This process will pull the wick through to the bottom of the candle.

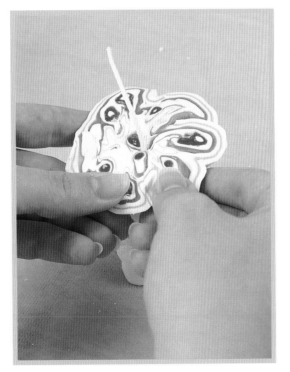

5 Squeeze the wax back together where the knife cut through and reform the mushroom.

6 Dip the candle into clear wax and then the glaze for the finishing touch.

Equipment Maintenance and Safety Precautions

Never leave melting wax unattended. Depending on the melting point of the particular wax you are using, it can ignite if heated to temperatures of 410°F (210°C) or above.

Always keep a towel or potholder handy to use for picking up hot containers.

Always have a fire extinguisher on hand.

When pouring wax, avoid spilling it onto the burner. If the wax spills or splashes out of its container and touches the heat source on the stove or hot plate, you are at risk of causing a fire. Wax may spill into the water container of your double-boiler system as you're stirring it. This is fine, as long as you clean it off once it cools. At the end of each candlemaking session, use paper towels to clean up any water or wax spills while the hot plate is still warm and the wax is soft. The wax in the water container of the double boiler will float to the top and harden as it cools, making it easy to remove from the water. Do NOT dump water with wax in it down any drain—wax will clog your plumbing.

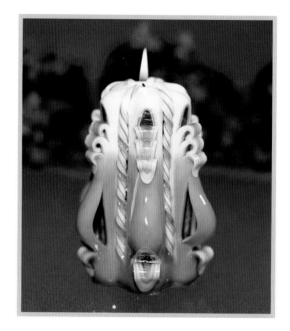

Pouring wax at the correct temperature and using the correct blend will help you avoid wax buildup in your candle molds. If you find that buildup has occurred, there are several methods for removing it. The first way is to use a wax remover, available from candlemaking suppliers, to clean the mold. Another method is to heat your oven to 150° to 170°F (65 to 76°C) and set the molds in the oven upside down on a foil-lined cookie tray. Use a tray with sides so that the wax doesn't melt into the oven. Most of the molds that you'll use for the core candles are star-shaped, and cleaning them with wax remover may be difficult, so this method would be a good alternative.

Cleaning your carving tools is simple. Just dip them in boiling water for a minute, and wipe them clean with a paper towel. This technique is especially beneficial to use before you begin each candle to give you a clean cut each time.

As with all candles, cut and carve candles should be stored in a cool place, away from direct sunlight and heat. Since cut and carve candles are delicate and fragile, it is important to protect them with tissue paper and bubble wrap before putting them in bins and boxes.

Troubleshooting

When you're first learning to make cut and carve candles, you may encounter some challenges until you get used to the techniques. As you gain experience, you'll become more skillful and probably develop your own approaches for dealing with difficulties in the candlemaking process. In the meantime, here's a list of potential problems and solutions for dealing with them.

Problem

Wick breaks as you're pulling the candle from the mold.

Solution

Put the candle in the freezer for about 45 minutes to 1 hour. Grip the remaining wick with needle-nose pliers, and pull the candle out of the mold. If the candle still doesn't come out, turn the mold upside down and hold onto the long wick used for dipping. Dip the entire mold and candle in boiling water. After a few minutes, remove it from the water and turn the candle over. Use pliers to pull the candle from the mold. Keep repeating until the candle comes free.

Problem

Layers of color separate when you carve the candle.

Solution

This problem arises when your wax is not correctly blended. If the wax you use is not 100 percent paraffin, it may contain additives that cause the layers to separate. You may need to blend in an additive called tacky wax or sculpture wax to your wax while melting. This will help the layers to adhere to each other.

Problem

The white layers are not distinctive.

Solution

Add more pigment or titanium white oil paint to your wax.

Problem

Colors are bleeding.

Solution

Be sure you are using pigment dyes and not regular candle dye. Adding a few more dips of white between layers may also help.

Problem

Glaze on finished candle looks spotty or uneven.

Solution

Remember to do a final dip in clear wax before applying the glaze. Be careful not to touch the candle between the clear wax and glaze step, as this will also cause spotting.

Problem

Wax strip falls off of candle while stretching candle or cutting the strip.

Solution

While the wax is still warm, reattach the strip to the candle by pressing it back in place until the wax blends into the candle.

Problem

The bottom of your candle is uneven.

Solution

Place the candle on a griddle or other flat, heated surface. Rub the candle back and forth until the uneven spots have melted off and the surface of the bottom is even.

⊡ COLUMN CANDLE

The shape of your core candle will have a big effect on the design you choose and the finished look of your candle. Experiment with a square core candle to discover the results you'll get with this distinctive shape.

Double-boiler system for
3 containers of wax

4-inch (10.2 cm) square
core candle

S hook

Clear wax

White pigment

Black pigment

Bucket of cool water

Carving station

Paring knife

Ribbon-carving tool

Wax paper

Candle glaze

Scissors

Copper tubing

PREPARING THE WAX

Prepare the wax as described on page 14. Set up your double boilers to accommodate the clear, white, and black wax. Test your colors before you begin, to ensure they are the desired shade or richness in color. Stir the pigment dyes thoroughly.

DIPPING PROCESS

1 Tie the core candle to the hook, and dip the candle into the white wax for approximately 45 seconds. Remove the candle from the wax, and dip it into the cool water bath. Remove it promptly and gently wipe off any excess water drops.

Continue dipping in the following color sequence:

4 dips of white

6 dips of black

5 dips of white

4 dips of black

5 dips of white

Remember to dip the candle into the water bath after every layer of wax.

CARVING PROCESS

2 Hang the candle at eye level for carving. Gather the excess drippings on bottom to use as a handle.

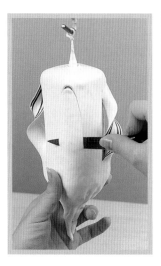  

3 Make a cut from one of the top corners down to about ½ inch (1.3 cm) from the bottom of the candle. Pull the strip of wax out, twist it a few times, then reattach it to the candle at the top of the cut. Repeat this process for each corner of the candle.

5 Cut the excess drippings off the bottom of the candle in a smooth, even motion. Place the candle on a smooth, flat surface, and level it with the palm of your hand.

SEALING THE CANDLE

Dip the finished candle into the clear wax to remove any oil residue left by your hands. Dip the candle in the glaze and hang it to let the excess glaze drip off. Blow off any air bubbles. After about 1 to 2 minutes (or until the glaze stops dripping off the candle), set candle on a flat surface protected with wax paper, and cut the wick from the hook. Use your copper tubing (or similar object) to remove the dipped layers of wax from around the wick.

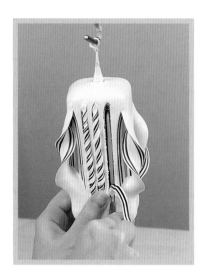

4 On each flat side of the candle, use your ribbon tool to make three gouges that start near the top of the candle and continue down to a position parallel to the end of the twist you made in step 3. For each cut, remove the ribbon tool from the strip of wax, twist the strip tightly, then reposition it in the original cut, and reattach the strip to the candle at the top.

BOW-TIE CANDLE

A little bow-tie candle dresses up your room delightfully. Once you've learned the technique, you'll just repeat it, creating row after row of bows.

- Double-boiler system for 4 containers of wax
- 4-inch-tall (10.2 cm) 6-point-star core candle
- S hook
- Clear wax
- White pigment
- Yellow pigment
- Black pigment
- Bucket of cool water
- Carving station
- Paring knife
- Ribbon-carving tool
- Candle glaze
- Wax paper
- Scissors
- Copper tubing

PREPARING THE WAX

Prepare the wax as described on page 14. Set up your double boilers to accommodate the clear, white, yellow, and black wax. Test your colors before you begin to ensure they are the desired shade or richness in color. Stir the pigment dyes thoroughly.

DIPPING PROCESS

1 Tie the core candle to the hook and dip the candle into the yellow wax for approximately 45 seconds. Remove the candle from the wax and dip it into the cool water bath. Remove it promptly and gently wipe off any excess water drops. Continue dipping, using the following color sequence:

4 dips of yellow

4 dips of white

4 dips of black

4 dips of white

4 dips of yellow

2 dips of black, two-thirds of the way up the candle (for a dark green effect)

Remember to dip the candle into the water bath after every layer of wax.

CARVING PROCESS

2 Hang the candle at eye level for carving. Gather the excess drippings on the bottom for your handle. Begin the first cut about 1 1/2 inches (3.8 cm) from the bottom. Fold the cut over and place the tip of the wax strip on the bottom of the candle, forming a lyre cut.

3 Make the second cut on each point of the star about 1/2 inch (1.3 cm) above the first. Fold one strip of wax downward into the center of the adjacent groove. Repeat for the strip on the next point so that the two strips meet in the center of the groove. Continue this same process on the remaining four points for a total of three bows.

4 Using the ribbon tool, make a gouge cut about ½ inch (1.3 cm) from the point where the folds meet in the center of the groove. Fold down the strip of wax to form a center for the "bow."

5 Repeat steps 3 and 4 to create a third and fourth row of bows.

6 When you've finished the rows of bows, there will be three remaining empty grooves in the candle. Starting at the top of the groove, use your ribbon tool to make a gouge cut all the way down to where the first row of bows starts. Remove the ribbon tool and twist your piece of wax several times, creating a spiral.

7 Reattach the strip of wax at the top of the groove.

Examine the candle to ensure that none of the strips have come loose. Cut off the handle in a smooth, even motion. Place the candle on a smooth, flat surface, and level it with the palm of your hand.

SEALING THE CANDLE

Dip the finished candle into the clear wax to remove any oil residue left by your hands. Dip the candle into the glaze and hang it from the S hook to let the excess glaze drip off. Blow off any air bubbles. After about 1 to 2 minutes (or until the glaze stops dripping off the candle), set the candle on a flat surface protected with wax paper and cut the wick from the hook. Use your copper tubing (or similar object) to remove the dipped layers of wax from around the wick.

RIBBONS *and* BOWS CANDLE

Like a fanciful Christmas confection or a beautifully wrapped present, this candle radiates good cheer. Combine twists, lyre cuts, and bows to achieve this effect.

You Will Need

Double-boiler system for 4 containers of wax

6-inch-tall (15.2 cm) 6-point-star core candle

S hook

Clear wax

White pigment

Red pigment

Green pigment

Bucket of cool water

Carving station

Paring knife

Ribbon-carving tool

Candle glaze

Wax paper

Scissors

Copper tubing

Preparing the Wax

Prepare the wax as described on page 14. Set up your double boilers to accommodate the clear, white, red and green wax. Stir the pigment dye thoroughly.

Dipping Process

1 Tie the candle to the hook and dip it into the white wax for approximately 45 seconds. Remove the candle from the wax and dip it into the cool water bath. Remove it promptly and gently wipe off any excess water drops. Continue dipping in the following sequence:

4 dips of white

5 dips of green

5 dips of white

3 dips of green

4 dips of white

5 dips of red

Remember to dip the candle into the water bath after every layer of wax.

Carving Process

2 Hang the candle at eye level for carving. Gather the excess drippings on the bottom for your handle. Holding the knife at about a 75° angle, make a cut about 2 inches (5 cm) from the bottom of the candle. Continue to make this same cut in the same position all the way around the candle. Fold each cut over and secure its tip to the candle.

3 Repeat this same cut, ³/₄ inch (1.9 cm) above the first all the way around the candle, rolling it down so it rests on top of the first cut.

4 Make another cut about 1 ½ inches (3.8 cm) from the top of the candle (or 2 inches [5.2 cm] above previous cut) all the way down to the previous cut. Repeat this process on each point of the candle. Fold one wax strip over, positioning its tip in the center of the groove between two points of the candle. Then fold the adjacent piece into the groove from the opposite direction so that the tips of the two pieces touch. Repeat the process for the remaining four wax strips.

5 The next two cuts, which are positioned close to the top of the candle, are made in the same way described in steps 2 and 3: the first cut folds over forming a lyre cut, the second rolls down.

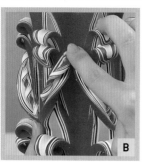

6 Firmly press the ribbon tool into the candle starting in a position just slightly to the left of one of the strips you folded over in step 4. Drag the tool down the length of the previous cut. Hold the wax strip with one hand and slide the tool off the strip. Twist the strip a few times, then position it inside the closest folded strip. Repeat the process for each set of folded strips.

7 Press the tool into the groove between two points of a star, starting parallel to the top of the top cut on the candle. Twist the strip as you pull it away from the candle, letting it curl into a knot. Press it back into the candle at the base of the cut.

8 Beginning under each knot, use the ribbon tool to make a gouge twist all the way down to the bottom of the candle.

Examine the candle to ensure everything is securely in place. Cut off the excess drippings, making sure that you cut evenly all around the candle. Place the candle on a smooth, flat surface and level it with the palm of your hand.

SEALING THE CANDLE

Dip the finished candle into the clear wax to remove any oil residue from your hands. Dip the candle in the glaze and let the excess glaze drip off. Wait 1 to 2 minutes, or until the glaze stops dripping off the candle, then set it on a flat surface protected with wax paper and cut the wick from the hook. Use your copper tubing (or similar object) to remove the dipped layers of wax from around the wick.

ROWS *of* BOWS CANDLE

Once you learn the bow technique, you can apply it to a number of different designs. This one includes a simple gouge twist for each row of bows.

YOU WILL NEED

Double-boiler system for
4 containers of wax

6-inch-tall (15.2 cm)
6-point-star core candle

S hook

Clear wax

White pigment

Cranberry pigment

Lavender pigment

Bucket of cool water

Carving station

Paring knife

Ribbon-carving tool

Candle glaze

Wax paper

Scissors

Copper tubing

PREPARING THE WAX

Prepare the wax as described on page
14. Set up your double boilers to accommodate the clear, white, cranberry, and lavender wax. Test your colors before you begin to ensure they are the desired shade or richness in color. Stir the pigment dyes thoroughly.

DIPPING PROCESS

1 Tie the core candle to the hook and dip candle into the lavender wax for approximately 45 seconds. Remove the candle from the wax and dip it into the cool water bath. Remove it promptly and gently wipe off any excess water drops. Continue dipping in the following color sequence:

4 dips of lavender

4 dips of white

4 dips of cranberry

4 dips of white

5 dips of lavender

Remember to dip the candle into the water bath after every layer of wax.

CARVING PROCESS

2 Hang the candle at eye level for carving. Gather the excess drippings on the bottom for your handle. Begin the first cut about 2 inches (5 cm) from the bottom. Do not fold the cut over, just bend it out until you've completed the second cut. Repeat the cut on each point of the star.

3 Make the second cut on each point of the star about ³/₄ inch (1.9 cm) above the first. Fold one strip of wax downward into the center of the adjacent groove. Do the same for the strip on the next point so that the two strips meet in the center of the groove. Repeat on the four remaining points of the candle for a total of three bows.

4 Next, take the first wax strip and stretch the wax upward in the opposite direction, forming an upward bow in the three remaining grooves of the candle.

5 Using the ribbon tool, make a gouge cut about 1 inch (2.5 cm) above the point where the folds meet in the center of the groove. Fold down the strip of wax to form a center for the "bow."

6 Create another two rows of cuts above the ones you made in steps 2 and 3. Repeat the process of folding the strips of wax into the center of the grooves between the star's points.

7 Repeat steps 2, 3, 4, and 5 to create a third row of bows.

Examine the candle to ensure that none of the strips have come loose. Cut off the handle in a smooth, even motion. Place the candle on a smooth, flat surface, and level it with the palm of your hand.

SEALING THE CANDLE

Dip the finished candle into the clear wax. Dip it into the glaze and hang it to let the excess glaze drip off. Blow off any air bubbles. After about 1 to 2 minutes (or until the glaze stops dripping off the candle), set the candle on a flat surface protected with wax paper and cut the wick from the hook. Use your copper tubing (or similar object) to remove the dipped layers of wax from around the wick.

CITRUS SPLASH
CANDLE

An appealing color scheme and ornate design make this candle a delight to look at.

You Will Need

Double-boiler system for 4 containers of wax

4-inch-tall (10.2 cm) 6-point-star core candle

S hook

Clear wax

White pigment

Sea green pigment

Yellow pigment

Bucket of cool water

Carving station

Paring knife

Ribbon-carving tool

Candle glaze

Wax paper

Scissors

Copper tubing

PREPARING THE WAX

Prepare the wax as described on page 14. Set up your double boilers to accommodate the clear, white, sea green, and yellow wax. Test your colors before you begin to ensure they are the desired shade or richness in color. Stir the pigment dyes thoroughly.

DIPPING PROCESS

1 Tie the core candle to the hook and dip the candle into the yellow wax for approximately 45 seconds. Remove the candle from the wax and dip it into the cool water bath. Remove it promptly and gently wipe off any excess water drops. Continue dipping in the following color sequence:

2 dips of yellow

4 dips of white

4 dips of sea green

4 dips of white

3 dips of yellow

5 dips of white

2 dips of green (only bottom two-thirds of candle, leaving the top white)

Remember to dip the candle into the water bath after every layer of wax.

CARVING PROCESS

2 Hang the candle at eye level for carving. Gather the excess drippings on the bottom to make a handle. First, do a lyre cut beginning about 1 inch (2.5 cm) from the bottom on each point of the candle.

3 Next, make a cut about 1 1/2 inches (3.8 cm) from the top of the candle all the way down to the bottom of the previous cut. Repeat on each point of the candle. Gently stretch the wax strip created by each cut, fold it over your finger, and attach it to the candle at the top of the cut.

4 Slightly above the tip that you just reattached to the candle, make a small lyre cut, then make a cut on top of that one, resting the tip of the wax strip on the top of the loop of the previous cut.

SEALING THE CANDLE

Dip the finished candle into the clear wax to remove any oil residue from your hands that might remain on the candle. Dip the candle in the glaze hang it to let the excess glaze drip off. Blow off any air bubbles. After about 1 to 2 minutes (or until the glaze stops dripping off the candle), set the candle on a flat surface protected by wax paper and cut the wick from the hook. Use your copper tubing (or similar object) to remove the dipped layers of wax from around the wick.

5 Use the ribbon-carving tool to make a gouge cut in the groove between two points in the candle. Remove the tool, tightly twist the wax strip, then place it back into the cut, pressing it in at the top. Repeat for the remaining grooves in the candle.

Examine the candle to ensure that none of the wax strips have come loose. Cut the excess drippings from the bottom of the candle in a smooth, even motion. Place the candle on a smooth, flat surface and level it with the palm of your hand.

DOUBLE LAYER
with a TWIST

Just like a beautiful multitiered wedding cake, this candle combines twists and lyre cuts to create a feast for the eyes. It's truly dazzling when lit, spreading a warm glow through its layers of twisted columns.

You Will Need

Double-boiler system for
4 containers of wax

6-inch-tall (15.2 cm)
6-point-star core candle

S hook

Clear wax

White pigment

Peach pigment

Brown pigment

Bucket of cool water

Carving station

Paring knife

Ribbon-carving tool

Candle glaze

Wax paper

Copper tubing

Preparing the Wax

Prepare the wax as described on page 14. Set up your double boilers to accommodate the clear, white, peach, and brown wax. Test your colors before you begin to ensure they are the desired shade or richness in color. Stir the pigment dyes thoroughly.

Dipping Process

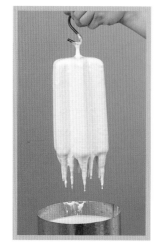

1 Tie the core candle to the hook and dip the candle into the white wax for approximately 45 seconds. Remove the candle from the wax and dip it into the cool water bath. Remove it promptly and gently wipe off any excess water drops. Continue dipping in the following color sequence:

5 dips of white

5 dips of peach

3 dips of white

3 dips of peach

5 dips of white

3 dips of brown

5 dips of white

Remember to dip the candle into the water bath after every layer of wax.

Carving Process

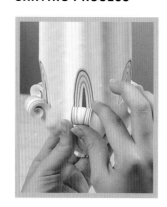

2 Hang the candle at eye level for carving. Gather the excess drippings on the bottom for a handle. Beginning 2 inches (5 cm) from the bottom of the candle, make a roll cut on all six points.

3 Begin the next cut about 1 1/2 inches (3.8 cm) above the first. Pull the wax strip out and twist it, then reattach it to the candle at the top of the cut. Repeat this process on each point of the candle.

4 Make a small lyre cut just above the top of the twist you just created. Repeat this process on each point of the candle.

5 Starting about 1 ½ inches (3.8 cm) above the lyre cut you just made, make a twist cut on each point of the candle, just as you did in step 3.

6 Make another lyre cut, just as you did in step 4, just above the twist you completed in step 5. Repeat on each point of the candle.

7 In the groove between two of the candle's star points, use your ribbon-cutting tool to make a gouge down the length of the candle, starting adjacent to the top lyre cut you just made and ending at the bottom of the first twist cut you made. Pull the strip of wax from the candle, twist it tightly, then place it back inside the groove. Repeat on every other groove of the candle for three times total.

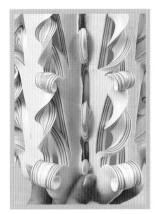

8 In the next groove of the candle, make three smaller gouge cuts with the ribbon tool, simply folding over the strip of wax to make a small tab with each strip of wax. Repeat on every other groove for three times total.

Examine the candle to ensure that none of the strips of wax have come loose. Cut off the excess drippings in a smooth, even motion. Place the candle on a smooth, flat surface and level it with the palm of your hand.

SEALING THE CANDLE

Dip the finished candle into the clear wax to remove any oil residue left by your hands. Dip the candle in the glaze and hang it to let the excess glaze drip off. Blow off any air bubbles. After about 1 to 2 minutes (or until the glaze stops dripping off the candle), set candle on a flat surface that's protected with wax paper and cut the wick from the hook. Use your copper tubing (or similar object) to remove the dipped layers of wax from around the wick.

BUTTERFLY
CANDLE

Delicate butterflies with fluttering wings grace the side of this candle. You'll enjoy seeing how they light up the night, glowing from within after they're lit.

PREPARING THE WAX

Prepare the wax as described on page 14. Set up your double boilers to accommodate the clear, white, silver, and cranberry wax. Test your colors before you begin to ensure they are the desired shade or richness in color. Stir the pigment dyes thoroughly.

DIPPING PROCESS

1 Tie the core candle to the hook and dip it into the silver wax for approximately 45 seconds. Remove the candle from the wax and dip it into the cool water bath. Remove it promptly and gently wipe off any excess water. Continue dipping in the following color sequence:

5 dips of silver

4 dips of white

5 dips of cranberry

5 dips of white

Remember to dip the candle into the water bath after every layer of wax.

CARVING PROCESS

2 Hang the candle at eye level for carving. Gather the excess drippings on the bottom to make a handle. Begin with the bottom butterfly. Make a 2-inch (5.2 cm) lyre cut near the bottom of two points of the candle.

3 Starting about 1 inch (2 cm) above the cut you made in step 2, make another cut above each of the previous cuts. Fold each cut out in opposite directions, placing the tip of the wax strip just outside the cut. These are the wings of the butterfly.

4 When you've finished making the wings, use the ribbon-carving tool to make a gouge cut in the groove in between the two wings. Fold the wax strip down. This is the butterfly's head. Create another butterfly using the same process, but position the butterfly on the adjacent two points, slightly higher up on the candle.

5 Make another butterfly further up on the two remaining points still higher up the candle. After you've made the gouge cut for the head, make the antennae. Use your ribbon-carving tool to make two small gouges in a V shape just above the head. Remove the wax strip completely from the candle. Repeat for the two other butterflies you made.

6 Using the ribbon-carving tool, make several light gouge cuts around the bottom of the candle.

Examine the candle to ensure that none of the wax strips have come loose. Cut the excess drippings from the bottom of the candle in a smooth, even motion. Place the candle on a smooth, flat surface and level it with the palm of your hand.

SEALING THE CANDLE

Dip the finished candle into the clear wax to remove any oil residue from your hands. Dip it in the glaze and hang it to let the excess glaze drip off. Blow off any air bubbles. After about 1 to 2 minutes (or until the glaze stops dripping off the candle), set the candle on a flat surface protected with wax paper and cut the wick from the hook. Use your copper tubing (or similar object) to remove the dipped layers of wax from around the wick.

· TWIST CANDLE

The twist is an easy-to-make, versatile cut that creates a surprisingly sophisticated look. Add several twists to a single candle for over-the-top elegance.

Double-boiler system for 4 containers of wax

10-inch-tall (25.4 cm) 6-point-star core candle

S hook

Clear wax

White pigment

Black pigment

Silver pigment

Bucket of cool water

Carving station

Paring knife

Ribbon-carving tool

Candle glaze

Wax paper

Scissors

Copper tubing

PREPARING THE WAX

Prepare the wax as described on page 14. Set up your double boilers to accommodate the clear, white, black, and silver wax. Test your colors before you begin to ensure they are the desired shade or richness in color. Stir the pigment dyes thoroughly.

DIPPING PROCESS

1 Tie the core candle to the hook and dip it into black wax for approximately 45 seconds. Remove candle from wax and dip it into the cool water bath. Remove it promptly and gently wipe off any excess water drops. Continue dipping in the following color sequence:

5 dips of black

3 dips of white

5 dips of silver

3 dips of white

4 dips of silver

1 dip of silver, halfway up

5 dips of black, one-third of the way up

Remember to dip the candle into the water bath after every layer of wax.

CARVING PROCESS

2 Hang the candle at eye level for carving. Gather the excess drippings on the bottom for your handle. The first cut is a 2 1/2-inch (6.4 cm) lyre cut, followed by two roll cuts on all six points of the candle. Each roll cut should begin about 1/2 inch (1.3 cm) above the previous one.

3 Beginning about 3 inches (7.6 cm) from the top of the candle (or 2 ½ inches [6.4 cm] above previous cut), make a 3-inch (7.6 cm) cut.

6 Make a tuck cut on top of the roll (this is similar to a roll cut, but it doesn't roll completely under because it rests on the top of the previous cut).

4 Twist each strip of wax you cut, then reattach it to the candle at the top of the cut. Twist each cut in the same direction.

7 In the groove between two points of the candle, use your ribbon tool to create a gouge from the top of the candle to the bottom of the twist cut you did in step 3.

5 Slightly over the cut you made in step 3, make a short lyre cut on each point of the candle. Fold the tip of the cut over the top of the twist cut. Follow that cut by a roll cut, above the lyre cut.

8 Pull the strip out and pull off the ribbon-cutting tool. Twist the strip and repeat the process between the points of each star.

9 Stretch your first twisted strip of wax over the adjacent twist cut.

SEALING THE CANDLE

Dip the finished candle into the clear wax to remove any oil residue from your hands. Dip the candle into the glaze and hang it to let the excess glaze drip off. Blow off any air bubbles. After about 1 to 2 minutes (or until the glaze quits dripping off the candle), set the candle on a flat surface protected by wax paper and cut the wick from the hook. Use your copper tubing (or similar object) to remove the dipped layers of wax from around the wick.

10 Reattach the strip to the candle near the wick. Repeat this process with each twisted strip of wax.

Examine the candle to ensure all the strips remain in place. Cut the excess drippings from the bottom of the candle in a smooth, even motion. Place the candle on a smooth, flat surface and level it with the palm of your hand.

BASKET WEAVE CANDLE

Woven from wax, the elaborate pattern at the base of this candle may look intimidating to the beginning candlemaker. But it's actually quite simple to create with a few basic cuts and twists.

YOU WILL NEED

Double-boiler system for 5 containers of wax

6-inch-tall (15.2 cm) 6-point-star core candle

S hook

Clear wax

White pigment

Red pigment

Orange pigment

Yellow pigment

Bucket of cool water

Carving station

Paring knife

Ribbon-carving tool

Candle glaze

Wax paper

Scissors

Copper tubing

PREPARING THE WAX

Prepare the wax as described on page 14. Set up your double boilers to accommodate clear, white, red, orange, and yellow wax. Be sure to test your colors before you begin to ensure they are the desired shade or richness in color. Stir the pigment dyes thoroughly.

DIPPING PROCESS

1 Tie the core candle to the S hook and dip the candle into the white wax for approximately 45 seconds. Remove the candle from the wax and dip it into the cool water bath. Remove it promptly and gently wipe off any excess water drops. Continue dipping in the following color sequence:

5 dips of white

5 dips of red

4 dips of white

5 dips of orange

4 dips of white

5 dips of yellow

5 dips of white

Remember to dip the candle into the water bath after every layer of wax. Depending on how many layers you do, you may need to wait for a couple minutes before beginning the carving process. This lets the wax cool enough to help the wax layers stick together.

CARVING PROCESS

2 Hang the candle at eye level for carving. Gather the excess drippings on the bottom for your handle. Begin with a 2 ½-inch (6.4 cm) lyre cut near the bottom of each point of the candle.

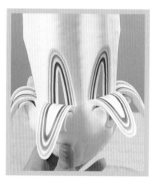

3 The next cut, which begins the basket design, should be about ³/₄ inch (1.9 cm) above the top of the first cut. Make a 2 ½-inch (6.4 cm cm) cut on each point of the candle.

4 Bend the first cut strip of wax over to touch the top of the lyre cut on the adjacent point of the candle. Take the strip of wax just above this folded piece and bend it to overlap the first piece, tucking it under. Continue folding and tucking the cuts on each point of the candle. This creates the first layer of the basket weave.

5 Begin the next cut about ³/₄ inch (1.9 cm) above the previous cut and fold each strip as you did with the previous row, but in the reverse direction.

6 Starting at the top of the candle, use your ribbon tool to make a gouge in the groove between two points of the star. Remove the tool from the strip of wax, then twist the strip and reattach it to the candle at the top of the cut.

7 Create another two layers of basket weave just as you did in steps 4 and 5.

8 Examine the candle to ensure that the strips of wax haven't come loose. Cut the excess drippings from the bottom of the candle in an even motion. Place the candle on a smooth, flat surface and level it with the palm of your hand.

SEALING THE CANDLE

Dip the finished candle into the clear wax to remove any oil residue from your hands. Dip the candle into the glaze and hang it to let the excess glaze drip off. Blow off any air bubbles. After about 1 to 2 minutes (or until the glaze stops dripping off the candle), set the candle on a flat surface protected with wax paper and cut the wick from the hook. Use your copper tubing (or similar object) to remove the dipped layers of wax from around the wick.

BASKET WEAVE
with a TWIST CANDLE

Combining three easy and eye-catching techniques, this candle has a stately, dramatic appearance. The beautiful color makes it appealing in the daytime, but it casts beautiful shadows when lit at night.

Double-boiler system for
3 containers of wax

10-inch-tall (25.4 cm)
6-point-star core candle

S hook

Clear wax

White pigment

Teal pigment

Bucket of cool water

Carving station

Paring knife

Ribbon-carving tool

Candle glaze

Wax paper

Scissors

Copper tubing

PREPARING THE WAX

Prepare the wax as described on page 14. Set up your double boilers to accommodate the clear, white, and teal wax. Test the colors before you begin to ensure they are the desired shade or richness in color. Stir the pigment dyes thoroughly.

DIPPING PROCESS

1 Tie the core candle to the S hook and dip the candle into the white wax for approximately 45 seconds. Remove the candle from wax and dip it into the cool water bath. Remove it promptly and gently wipe off any excess water drops. Continue dipping in the following color sequence:

5 dips of white

3 dips of clear

4 dips of white

3 dips of teal

5 dips of white

3 dips of teal

Remember to dip the candle into the water bath after every layer of wax.

CARVING PROCESS

2 Hang the candle at eye level for carving. Gather the excess drippings on the bottom to make a handle. Begin with a lyre cut on the point of each star about 2 1/2 inches (6.4 cm) from the bottom of the candle.

3 Next, make a 4-inch (10.2 cm) cut on each point above the first cut.

4 Twist each strip of wax created in step 3, then reattach it to the candle at the top of the cut.

7 Fold one strip of wax on one point over to touch the tip of the lyre cut on the adjacent point. Repeat this process for all the strips of wax, creating a basket weave pattern.

5 Make a small lyre cut right above the point where you reattached the twist. Firmly place the bottom of the lyre over the tip of the twist. This helps prevent the twist from falling off.

8 Make another layer of basket weave cuts in the opposite direction over the one you created in steps 6 and 7.

6 Above the lyre cut, make a cut approximately 2 inches (5 cm) long. Repeat for each point of the candle.

9 If you have room, do an additional layer of basket weave cuts on top of the previous one.

10 Using the ribbon tool, make a gouge twist in the groove between two points of the candle starting at the point below the basket weave and ending near the top of the lyre cut at the bottom of the candle. Repeat this on every other groove of the candle for a total of three times.

11 Using the ribbon tool, make a gouge cut in each of the three remaining grooves, starting at the point below the basket weave and ending halfway down the twist. Fold the wax strip out and attach the tip near the bottom of the twist cut.

Examine the candle to ensure that the wax strips have not come loose. Cut the excess drippings from the bottom of the candle in a smooth, even motion. Place the candle on a smooth, flat surface and level it with the palm of your hand.

Sealing the Candle

Dip the finished candle into the clear wax to remove any oil residue left by your hands. Dip it into the glaze and hang to let the excess glaze drip off. Blow off any air bubbles. After about 1 to 2 minutes (or until the glaze stops dripping off the candle), set the candle on a flat surface protected with wax paper and cut the wick from the hook. Use your copper tubing (or similar object) to remove the dipped layers of wax from around the wick.

HEART CANDLE

A perfect gift for a friend or sweetheart, this sweet candle is sure to be cherished. It's a good design for practicing your basic cuts, plus learning a few new tricks.

YOU WILL NEED

Double-boiler system for
4 containers of wax

10-inch-tall (25.4 cm)
6-point-star core candle

S hook

Clear wax

White pigment

Cranberry pigment

Lavender pigment

Bucket of cool water

Carving station

Paring knife

Ribbon-carving tool

Candle glaze

Wax paper

Scissors

Copper tubing

PREPARING THE WAX

Prepare the wax as described on
page 14. Set up your double
boilers to accommodate the clear,
white, cranberry, and lavender
wax. Test your colors before you
begin to ensure they are the
desired shade or richness in color.
Stir the pigment dyes thoroughly.

DIPPING PROCESS

1 Tie the core candle to the hook and dip the
candle in the cranberry wax for approximately
45 seconds. Remove the candle from the wax and
dip it into the cool water bath. Remove it promptly
and gently wipe off any excess water drops off.
Continue dipping in the following color sequence:

4 dips of cranberry

4 dips of white

3 dips of cranberry

4 dips of white

2 dips of lavender

3 dips of white

2 dips of lavender

Remember to dip the candle into the water
bath after every layer of wax.

CARVING PROCESS

2 Near the bottom of each star
point, make a cut about 2 1/2
inches (5.2 cm) long, then slice that
cut down the center vertically.

3 Twist each half of the cut
strip slightly, then fold each
one outward into the adjacent groove
of the candle so that it meets the
strip from the adjacent star point.

4 Next, make a lyre cut
about 1 1/2 inches
(3.8 cm) above the first cut.

5 On two points of the candle (front and back), make a roll cut over the lyre cut you made in step 3. Starting from the top of the candle, make a cut that ends slightly above the roll cut. Slice the strip of wax in half, then stretch and fold each piece into the center of the cut to form a heart. Repeat the heart cut on the back side of the candle.

6 On each of the four remaining points of the candle, make a cut about 1 1/2 inches (3.8 cm) above the lyre cut you made in step 3. Twist the strip of wax from the cut, twist in, then reattach it to the candle at the top of the cut.

7 On each point of the candle except the ones with the heart, make a lyre cut above the twist cut you made in step 5. Over each lyre cut, make a roll cut that rests on the top of the lyre cut.

8 In the groove between two points of the candle, use your ribbon tool to make a gouge cut that starts adjacent to the top of the uppermost roll cut and ends adjacent to the top of the twist cut. Pull the strip of wax down and fold it over.

9 Use your ribbon-cutting tool to make a gouge in all the grooves, beginning about 1 inch (2.5 cm) above the cuts in step 2 and ending at the top of that cut.

10 Pull each wax strip down, twist it into a knot, then press it back into the candle.

Examine the candle to make sure no wax strips have come loose. Cut off the excess drippings from the bottom of the candle in a smooth, even motion. Place the candle on a smooth, flat surface and push it down with the palm of your hand to level it.

SEALING THE CANDLE

Dip the finished candle into the clear wax to remove oil residue left by your hands. Dip it in the glaze and hang it on the S hook to let the glaze drip off. Blow off any air bubbles. After about 1 to 2 minutes (or until the glaze stops dripping), set the candle on a flat surface protected by wax paper and cut the wick from the hook. Use the copper tubing (or similar object) to remove the dipped layers of wax from around the wick.

DOUBLE-BOW
WEDDING CANDLE

The ultimate in elegance, this candle design is often used as the unity candle in weddings. Don't let the richly decorated appearance fool you—it's not difficult to make. You'll use all the familiar cuts, combined in new ways.

PREPARING THE WAX

Prepare the wax as described on page 14. Set up your double boilers to accommodate the clear and white wax. Stir the white pigment thoroughly.

DIPPING PROCESS

1 Tie the core candle to the hook and dip the candle into the white wax for approximately 45 seconds. Remove candle from wax and dip into the cool water bath. Remove promptly and gently wipe off any excess water drops. Continue dipping in the following color sequence:

5 dips of white

4 dips of clear

5 dips of white

3 dips of clear

5 dips of white

Remember to dip the candle into the water bath after every layer of wax.

CARVING PROCESS

2 Hang the candle at eye level for carving. Gather the excess drippings on the bottom to make a handle. **Note:** Since the container used to make this candle wasn't much taller than the core candle, there wasn't much room for drippings, so it was hard to create a handle at the bottom. Begin by making a 2-inch (5 cm) cut on all six points of the candle. Fold the wax strips over and let hang until later.

3 Make a second cut about 1 ½ inches (3.8 cm) above the first, ending halfway down the first cut.

4 Fold each wax strip created by the cut you made in step 3 into the groove adjacent to the cut so that each strip meets the adjacent strip in the middle of the groove.

5 Now fold the strips created by the cuts you made in step 2 in the opposite direction.

6 Make a row of small cuts above the top of the cuts you made in step 3. Fold the strips downward so that their tips rest on top of the tips of the first cuts (step 2).

7 The fourth cut is done about ½ inch (1.3 cm) above the third and is folded down toward the center groove where the second cut is placed. Once you fold all six of these points down, you will have a total of six bows around the candle.

8 Repeat steps 2 through 7 to make another set of bows on the top half of the candle. Begin the first cut of this step ½ inch (1.3 cm) above the previous cut.

SEALING THE CANDLE

Dip the finished candle into the clear wax to remove any oil from your hands. Dip the candle into the glaze and hang it to let the excess glaze drip off. Blow off any air bubbles. After about 1 to 2 minutes (or until the glaze quits stops off the candle), set the candle on a flat surface protected with wax paper, and cut the wick from the hook. Use your copper tubing (or similar object) to remove the dipped layers of wax from around the wick.

9 Using the ribbon tool, make a gouge knot above the center of each bow for a total of 12.

10 Finally, if you have enough room, make a gouge twist in the groove beneath the center of a bow. Repeat for the other bows.

Examine the candle to ensure none of the wax strips have come loose. Cut the excess drippings from the bottom of the candle in a smooth, even motion. Place the candle on a smooth, flat surface and level it with the palm of your hand.

FIRECRACKER
CANDLE

The colorful layers of this unusual candle resemble the beautiful sparks of a fireworks display. When lit, it glows dramatically from within, creating its own fantastic light show for your table, porch, or deck.

YOU WILL NEED

Double-boiler system for 4 containers of wax

10-inch-tall (25.4 cm) 6-point-star core candle

S hook

Clear wax

White pigment

Red pigment

Blue pigment

Bucket of cool water

Carving station

Paring knife

Candle glaze

Wax paper

Scissors

Copper tubing

PREPARING THE WAX

Prepare the wax as described on page 14. Set up your double boilers to accommodate the clear, white, red, and blue wax. Test your colors before you begin to ensure they are the desired shade or richness in color. Stir the pigment dyes thoroughly.

DIPPING PROCESS

1 Tie the core candle to the hook and dip candle into the clear wax for approximately 45 seconds. Remove the candle from the wax and dip it into the cool water bath. Remove it and gently wipe off any excess water drips. Continue dipping in the following sequence:

5 dips of red, four-fifths of the way to the top
5 dips of white
4 dips of red, four-fifths of the way to the top
5 dips of white
2 dips of blue

Remember to dip the candle into the water bath after every layer of wax.

CARVING PROCESS

2 Hang the candle at eye level for carving. Gather the excess drippings on the bottom for your handle. The first cut is a 1-inch (2.5 cm) roll that starts near the center of the candle on all six points.

3 Make an upward cut on each point of the candle, starting about 2 inches (5 cm) from the bottom and ending about 1/2 inch (1.3 cm) under each roll cut.

4 On each point of the candle, stretch the wax strip from the upward cut over the roll cut and reattach it to the candle.

5 Next, start at the bottom of the candle and make an upward cut on each point of the candle. Stretch out the wax strip and bow it outward with your finger. Then reattach the strip to the candle near the bottom of the cut.

6 Just over the top of the strip you attached in step 4, make a small lyre cut on each point of the star.

7 Create another row of cuts on top of the layer you created in step 6. Curve the wax strip over and place it on the tip of the previous roll.

8 Repeat step 7 again for an additional row of cuts.

Examine the candle to ensure that the strips of wax have not come loose. Cut off the excess drippings in a smooth, even motion. Place the candle on a smooth, flat surface and level it with the palm of your hand.

SEALING THE CANDLE

Dip the finished candle into the clear wax to remove any oil residue left by your hands. Dip it into the glaze and hang it to let the excess glaze drip off. Blow off any air bubbles. After about 1 to 2 minutes (or until the glaze stops dripping off the candle), set the candle on a flat surface that's protected by wax paper, and cut the wick from the hook. Use your copper tubing (or similar object) to remove the dipped layers of wax from around the wick.

LAYERED LYRE
CANDLE

This fantastic-looking candle displays what's best about cut and carve candles. It's lavishly decorated and wonderful to look at, but truly easy to make if you take it step by step.

YOU WILL NEED

Double-boiler system for
4 containers of wax

10-inch-tall (25.4 cm)
6-point-star core candle

S hook

Clear wax

White pigment

Orange pigment

Gold pigment

Bucket of cool water

Carving station

Paring knife

Ribbon-carving tool

Candle glaze

Wax paper

Scissors

Copper tubing

PREPARING THE WAX

Prepare the wax as described on page
14. Set up your double boilers to
accommodate the clear, white, orange,
and gold wax. Test your colors before
you begin to ensure they are the
desired shade or richness in color.
Stir the pigment dyes thoroughly.

DIPPING PROCESS

1 Tie the core candle to the hook and dip the candle into the orange wax for approximately 45 seconds. Remove the candle from the wax and dip it into the cool water bath. Remove promptly and gently wipe off any excess water drops. Continue dipping in the following color sequence:

4 dips of orange

4 dips of white

3 dips of gold

4 dips of white

1 dip of orange

1 dip of orange, two-thirds of the way up the candle

1 dip of orange, one-third of the way up the candle

Remember to dip the candle into the water bath after every layer of wax.

CARVING PROCESS

2 Hang the candle at eye level for carving. Gather the excess drippings at the bottom to use as a handle. The first cut is a ½-inch (1.3 cm) roll near the center of the candle. Repeat this cut on each point of the candle.

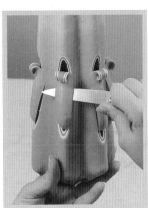

3 Next, make an upward cut that starts about 1 ½ inches (3.8 cm) from the bottom of the candle and ends just below the bottom of the roll cut.

4 Gently stretch the strips of wax from the cut in step 3 up and over the roll cut, reattaching the strips to the candle.

7 Twist the two pieces of each strip in opposite directions, then reattach them to the candle at the bottom of the cut.

5 Next, make an upward cut from the bottom of the candle to the bottom of the cut you just completed. Repeat the cut on each point of the candle.

8 Do a roll cut at the top of each upward lyre cut.

6 Cut each wax strip you created in step 5 in half.

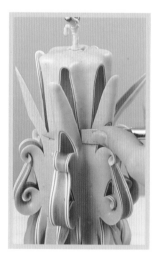

9 Make a cut starting at the top of each point of the candle and ending at the roll cut you created in step 8.

10 Slice each piece of wax from the cut in half, twist them in opposite directions, then reattach them at the top of the cut.

11 Using the ribbon-carving tool, make a gouge cut in the groove adjacent to the twists you completed in step 10. Bend the wax strip over and reattach it to the candle. Repeat for the other grooves in the candle.

12 Do two more, longer gouge cuts in each groove, bending over the wax strip created by the cut and reattaching it to the candle.

Examine the candle to make sure none of the wax strips have come loose. Cut the excess drippings off the bottom of the candle in a smooth, even motion. Place the candle on a smooth, flat surface and level it with the palm of your hand.

SEALING THE CANDLE

Dip the finished candle into the clear wax to remove any oil residue left by your hands. Next, dip it into the glaze and hang it to let the excess glaze drip off. Blow off any air bubbles. After about 1 to 2 minutes (or until the glaze stops dripping off the candle), set the candle on a flat surface protected with wax paper and cut the wick from the hook. Use your copper tubing (or similar object) to remove the dipped layers of wax from around the wick.

ANGEL CANDLE

Sparkling angel wings flutter on the side of this sweet and special candle. Just add a touch of glitter to the glaze for extra shine.

You Will Need

Double-boiler system for 2 containers of wax

4-inch-tall (10.2 cm) 6-point-star core candle

S hook

Clear wax

White pigment

Bucket of cool water

Carving station

Paring knife

Ribbon-carving tool

Candle glaze

Glitter

Wax paper

Scissors

Copper tubing

Preparing the Wax

Prepare the wax as described on page 14. Set up your double boilers to accommodate the clear and white wax. Stir the white pigment thoroughly.

Dipping Process

1 Tie the core candle to the hook and dip the candle into the white wax for approximately 45 seconds. Remove the candle from the wax and dip it into the cool water bath. Remove it promptly and gently wipe off any excess water drops. Continue dipping, using the following color sequence:

5 dips of white

4 dips of clear

4 dips of white

4 dips of clear

5 dips of white

Remember to dip the candle into the water bath after every layer of wax.

Carving Process

2 Hang the candle at eye level for carving. Gather the excess drippings on the bottom for your handle. Begin the first cut about 1 1/2 inches (3.8 cm) from the bottom on only two opposite sides of the candle. Fold the two cuts over and place the tip of the wax strip on the bottom of the candle, forming a lyre cut.

3 Create a twist cut beginning about 1/2 inch (1.3 cm) from the top of the candle and then another small lyre cut.

4 On the remaining four points, about one-third of the way from the top of the candle, make a 1/2 inch (1.3 cm) cut and fold each piece inward to meet each other.

5 Above the cuts made in step 4, make a cut that starts at the top of the candle and ends just above the previous cut. Fold each piece of wax out and place the tip in the adjacent groove. These are the wings.

8 Using the ribbon tool, make a gouge cut in the groove between both wings that extends from the top of the candle all the way to the bottom of the wings. Loop the strip over and attach the tip to the bottom of the gouge. This forms the head.

6 The next cut is an upward cut, which starts about 1 inch (2.5 cm) from the bottom all the way up to the bottom of the cut made in step 5. Repeat on all four points of the candle.

9 The final cuts are upward cuts that begin at the bottom and extend up under the cuts made in step 7. Do this on all four points. Use caution not to cut the strip off. Two at a time, stretch them out uniformly and bring the tips together in the center creating the "dress."

7 Fold each of these upward and place the tips in the grooves under the wings.

Examine the candle to ensure that none of the strips have come loose. Cut off the handle in a smooth, even motion. Place the candle on a smooth, flat surface and level it with the palm of your hand.

Sealing the Candle

Dip the finished candle into the clear wax to remove any oil residue left by your hands. Dip the candle into the glaze and hang it from the S hook to let the excess glaze drip off. Blow off any air bubbles. After about 1 to 2 minutes (or until the glaze stops dripping off the candle), set the candle on a flat surface protected with wax paper, sprinkle a little glitter on the candle and cut the wick from the hook. Use your copper tubing (or similar object) to remove the dipped layers of wax from around the wick.

DELIGHTFUL DECALS

With a simple slice of your knife, you can remove points from a star-shaped core candle and create a flat surface on your candle. What you do with that surface is up to you. Why not decorate it with seasonal or decorative decals that send a meaningful message?

YOU WILL NEED

Double-boiler system for
4 containers of wax

6-inch-tall (15.2 cm)
6-point-star core candle

S hook

Clear wax

White pigment

Gold pigment

Green pigment

Bucket of cool water

Carving station

Paring knife

Ribbon-carving tool

Decals

Candle glaze

Wax paper

Scissors

Copper tubing

PREPARING THE WAX

Prepare the wax as described on page 14. Set up your double boilers to accommodate the clear, white, gold, and green wax. Test your colors before you begin to ensure they are the desired shade or richness in color. Stir the pigment dyes thoroughly.

PREPARING THE CORE CANDLE

For this candle, you'll need to take a few extra steps before you start the dipping process. Tie the core to the S hook and hold it in clear wax for about 1 minute. Quickly dip it into the water and hang it at eye level. Using your knife, start a cut at the top of one star point of the candle and cut off the point all the way to the bottom. Dip the candle and hold it in clear wax again for about 30 seconds and cut the same strip again. Repeat this process until you have a smooth surface between two star points.

DIPPING PROCESS

Tie the core candle to the hook and dip it into gold wax for approximately 45 seconds. Remove the candle from the wax and dip it into the cool water bath. Remove promptly and gently wipe off any excess water drops. Continue dipping using the following color formula:

4 dips of gold

5 dips of white

6 dips of green

4 dips of white

3 dips of gold

5 dips of white

Remember to dip the candle into the water bath after every layer of wax.

CARVING PROCESS

2 Hang the candle at eye level for carving. Gather the excess drippings on the bottom for your handle. Begin with a 2-inch (5 cm) lyre cut near the bottom of each point of the candle.

3 Just above the top of the lyre cut, make a roll cut, resting the roll on the top of the lyre cut. Repeat on each point of the candle.

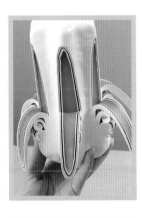

4 Starting about 1 1/2 inches (3.8 cm) from the top of each point on the candle, make a long cut that ends just above the lyre cut you made in step 3.

5 Pull out the strip of wax, twist it, then reattach it to the candle at the top of the cut.

6 Just above the top of the twist cut you made in steps 4 and 5, make a small lyre cut on each point of the candle.

7 In the groove in between two points of the candle, use your ribbon-carving tool to make a gouge running from the top of the candle to the spot adjacent to the bottom of the twist cut. Remove the ribbon tool, then twist the strip of wax tightly, and reattach the strip to the candle inside the groove. Repeat in each groove of the candle.

8 Attach your first decal to the flat side of the candle.

9 Attach another decal above the first. Continue adding decals to the flat side of the candle as space permits.

Examine the candle to make sure none of the wax strips have come loose. Cut the excess drippings from the bottom of the candle in a smooth, even motion. Place the candle on a smooth, flat surface and level it with the palm of your hand.

Sealing the Candle

Dip the finished candle into the clear wax to remove any oil residue left by your hands. Dip it into the glaze and hang it to let the excess glaze drip off. Blow off any air bubbles. After about 1 to 2 minutes (or until the glaze quits dripping off the candle), set the candle on a flat surface protected by wax paper and cut the wick from the hook. Use your copper tubing (or similar object) to remove the dipped layers of wax from around the wick.

LIGHTHOUSE
CANDLE

Glowing in a dimly lit room or on a porch or deck, this little lighthouse is a welcoming beacon. The "waves" at the bottom of the candle are created with a special, easy-to-do technique.

YOU WILL NEED

Double-boiler system for
4 containers of wax

4-inch-tall (10.2 cm)
6-point-star core candle

S hook

Clear wax

White pigment

Blue pigment

Green pigment

Bucket of cool water

Carving station

Paring knife

Ribbon-carving tool

Small shells

Small starfish

Candle glaze

Wax paper

Scissors

Copper tubing

PREPARING THE WAX

Prepare the wax as described on page 14. Set up your double boilers to accommodate the clear, white, blue, and green wax. Test your colors before you begin to ensure they are the desired shade or richness in color. Stir the pigment dyes thoroughly.

DIPPING PROCESS

1 Tie the core candle to the hook and dip the candle into the blue wax for approximately 45 seconds. Remove the candle from the wax and dip it into the cool water bath. Remove it promptly and gently wipe off any excess water drops. Continue dipping in the following color sequence:

4 dips of blue

4 dips of white

1 dip of blue

1 dip of green

1 dip of blue

1 dip of green

4 dips of white

4 dips of green

5 dips of white

1 dip of blue, two-thirds of the way up the candle

1 dip of green, one-third of the way up the candle

Remember to dip the candle into the water bath after every layer of wax. It is important that you have plenty of excess wax for this type of candle. If needed, add more layers.

CARVING PROCESS

2 Hang the candle at eye level for carving and gather the excess drippings on the candle in your hand.

3 Cut the excess drippings from the candle in a smooth, even motion.

4 Squeeze, mash, and stretch the wax.

5 Strech the excess drippings into a strip.

6 Stretch the wax all the way around the bottom of the candle (you may or may not need to use the whole handle). Mash it onto the candle to ensure that it stays in place. If it seems to be falling apart too much and sticking to your hands, it may be too hot. Set it down and let it cool for a short time before trying again.

7 Make a ½-inch (1.3 cm) cut on the top of each of the six points of the candle. Cut off each strip completely.

8 Use the ribbon tool to make gouges in a V shape on the candle. Twist the wax strips and position them slightly outside of the cut, then reaattach the strips to the candle near the top of the cut. Repeat this process in several positions around the candle.

9 Add your shells and starfish to the base of the candle in the design of your choice.

Examine the candle to ensure that the strips of wax remain in place and the shells and starfish are still attached. Put the candle on a smooth, flat surface and level it with the palm of your hand.

SEALING THE CANDLE

Dip the finished candle into the clear wax to remove any oil residue from your hands that may remain on the candle. Dip the candle into the glaze and hang it to let the excess glaze drip off. Blow off any air bubbles. After about 1 to 2 minutes (or until the glaze stops dripping off the candle), set the candle on a flat surface that's protected with wax paper and cut the wick from the hook. Use your copper tubing (or similar object) to remove the dipped layers of wax from around the wick.

NAUTICAL CANDLE

This distinctive candle combines unexpected techniques and unusual embellishments for a unique look. But don't let the remarkable appearance prevent you from giving it a try. It's easy to make with a few techniques you haven't seen until now.

PREPARING THE WAX

Prepare the wax as described on page 14. Set up your double boilers to accommodate the clear, white, blue, and green wax. Test your colors before you begin to ensure they are the desired shade or richness in color. Stir the pigment dyes thoroughly.

DIPPING PROCESS

1 Tie the candle to the hook and dip it into the blue wax for approximately 45 seconds. Remove the candle from the wax and dip it into the cool water bath. Remove it promptly from the water and gently wipe off any excess water drops. Continue dipping in the following color sequence:

1 dip of green

1 dip of blue

1 dip of green

1 dip of blue

4 dips of white

4 dips of blue

4 dips of white

4 dips of green

4 dips of white

1 dip of blue

1 dip of blue, half of candle

1 dip of green, one-fourth of the candle

Remember to dip the candle into the water bath after every layer of wax. It is important that you have plenty of excess drippings for this type of candle. If needed, add more layers.

CARVING PROCESS

2 Hang the candle at eye level for carving. Gather the excess drippings on the candle and cut them off. Squeeze, mash, and stretch the wax. Wrap the wax around the base of the candle.

3 Dig your finger or thumb into the center of the candle until you reach the core candle.

4 Gently fold the wax away from the core candle until you have an opening the size you want.

5 Fold the center wax over to blend with the rest of the wax.

6 Insert the large scallop shell into the center of the opening, pushing the bottom of the shell into the wax to secure it in place. If using glass embellishments, insert it at this time too, while the wax is still warm enough to hold it in place.

7 In the center of the opposite side of the candle, use the ribbon tool to make six gouge twists. The ones in the center should be the longest, and the ones radiating out from the center get progressively shorter. After removing the ribbon tool from each strip, twist the strip then reattach it to the candle just to the side of the gouge.

8 Near the top of the candle to each side of the central gouge twist design, make a small gouge and reattach the wax strip just to the side of the gouge. These are the seagulls or sea birds.

9 Add the rest of your embellishments to the candle in the design of your choice.

10 Examine the candle to ensure that all the wax strips remain in place. Place the candle on a smooth, flat surface and level it with the palm of your hand.

SEALING THE CANDLE

Dip the finished candle into the clear wax to remove any oil residue left by your hands that may remain on the candle. Dip the candle in the glaze and let it hang so that the excess glaze drips off. Blow off any air bubbles. After about 1 to 2 minutes (or until the glaze stops dripping), set the candle on a flat surface protected by wax paper and cut the wick from the hook. Use your copper tubing (or similar object) to remove the dipped layers of wax from around the wick.

◨ Bunny-*in*-*a*-Basket Candle

Transform an ordinary candle into a whimsical bunny with just a few twists and curls. This bunny makes a unique Easter gift or centerpiece for an Easter table setting.

You Will Need

Double-boiler system for
4 containers of wax

6-inch-tall (15.2 cm)
6-point-star core candle

S hook

Clear wax

White pigment

Green pigment

Blue pigment

Bucket of cool water

Carving station

Paring knife

Ribbon-carving tool

Google-eye embellishments*

Black bead*

Candle glaze

Wax paper

Scissors

Copper tubing

White cotton pom-pom*

White-tipped pin

Blue ribbon*

Hot glue gun and glue sticks*

*Available at craft stores

Preparing the Wax

Prepare the wax as described on page 14.
Set up your double boilers to accommodate
the clear, white, green, and blue wax.
Test your colors before you begin to ensure
they are the desired shade or richness in
color. Stir the pigment dyes thoroughly.

Dipping Process

1 Tie the core candle to the hook and dip the
candle into the blue wax for approximately
45 seconds. Remove the candle from the wax and
dip it into the cool water bath. Remove it promptly
and gently wipe off any excess water drops.
Continue dipping in the following color sequence:

4 dips of blue

5 dips of white

4 dips of blue

6 dips of white

1 dip of green on bottom one-third the
way up of candle

2 dips of green just below the first green
(to give it a layered look)

Remember to dip the candle into the water
bath after every layer of wax.

Carving Process

2 Hang the candle at eye level for carving.
Gather the excess drippings on the
bottom for a handle. Beginning 2 inches
(5 cm) from the bottom of the candle, do a lyre
cut on all six points.

3 Make another cut on each point of
the candle about 2 inches (5 cm)
from the top of the lyre cut.

4 Fold one strip over to the top of the lyre cut on the adjacent point. Continue folding each strip over to the adjacent point.

7 Just below the ears you created in step 6, push two google eyes into the wax. Just below and in between the eyes, push a black bead into the wax for the nose.

5 Make another cut on each point of the candle about 1 ¹/₂ inches (3.8 cm) above the previous cut. Fold each strip in the direction opposite the fold made in the previous layer and tuck it under the strip below. Repeat the process on all points of the candle to form the basket.

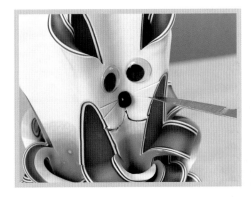

8 With the tip of your knife, make two cuts for the mouth. Slide the tip of the knife down and out for each side. Make the whiskers by sliding the knife from the nose out to form a light line.

6 To form the ears, make a 2-inch (5 cm) cut near the top of the candle on only two of the points. Fold each strip out and place in the adjacent groove, facing outward.

9 Examine the candle to ensure that the strips of wax have not come loose. Using your knife, cut off the excess drippings in a smooth, even motion. Place the candle on a smooth, flat surface and level it with the palm of your hand.

SEALING THE CANDLE AND ADDING EMBELLISHMENTS

Dip the finished candle into the clear wax to remove any oil residue left by your hands. Dip the candle into the glaze and hang it to let the excess glaze drip off. Blow off any air bubbles. After about 1 to 2 minutes (or until the glaze stops dripping off the candle), set the candle on a flat surface protected by wax paper and cut the wick from the hook. Use your copper tubing (or similar object) to remove the dipped layers of wax from around the wick.

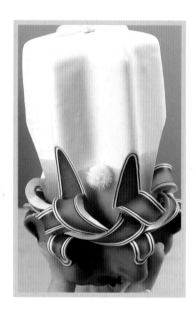

10 While the glaze is still drying, attach the pom-pom tail to the back side of the bunny with a white-tipped pin. Use caution to avoid putting your fingerprints on the drying glaze. Hold the candle by the wick with one hand and use your other hand to push on the tail.

11 After the candle has dried, hot glue the bow to the front of the bunny just above the basket.

TAPER
CANDLE

For a simple, elegant look, try a twist on a taper candle. Rather than hanging the candle from a hook, you'll use your hands or a taper holder as you carve. The finished product is a refined and graceful candle that's popular at weddings.

You Will Need

Double-boiler system for
3 containers of wax

10-inch-tall (25.4 cm)
white taper candle

Clear wax

White pigment

Yellow pigment

Wax paper

Candle glaze

Bucket of cool water

Paring knife

Taper holder (optional)

Scissors

Preparing the Wax

Prepare the wax as described on page 14. Set up your double boilers to accommodate the clear, white, and yellow wax. Test your colors before you begin to ensure they are the desired shade or richness in color. Stir the pigment dyes thoroughly.

Dipping Process

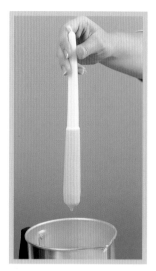

1 Mark the taper with your knife about one-third of the way from the bottom of the candle. This is where you will stop on each dip of wax except for the final dip. When first learning how to dip taper candles, use your hands instead of a taper holder. If you have a taper holder, pin the wick to it securely. Dip the taper into white wax up to your mark for approximately 30 seconds. Remove the candle from the wax and dip it into the cool water bath. Remove it promptly and gently wipe off any excess water drops. Continue dipping in the following color sequence:

4 dips of white

4 dips of yellow

4 dips of white

3 dips of clear

4 dips of white

1 dip of white for the entire taper

Remember to dip the candle into the water bath after every layer of wax.

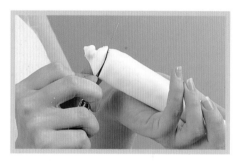

2 Once you are finished with the dipping process, cut the excess drippings off of the bottom.

CARVING PROCESS

3 Shave the bottom of the candle with your knife so that it will fit into a candleholder. It may help to have one nearby to help form it.

4 Just above the bottom, make four ½-inch (1.3 cm) lyre cuts around the candle, spacing the cuts out uniformly.

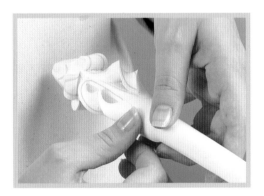

5 Starting about 1 ½ inches (3.8 cm) from the top of each lyre cut, make another cut. Pull the strip of wax out, then twist it, and reattach it to the candle at the top of the cut.

6 Make another lyre cut above each twist cut that you made in step 5.

Examine the candle to ensure that the strips haven't come loose.

SEALING THE CANDLE

Dip the finished candle into the clear wax, only to the top of the carved area. Don't dip the entire taper in the glaze, as this would inhibit proper burning. Let the excess glaze drip off. Blow off any air bubbles. Keep the candle upright while it dries.

Acknowledgments

As with any group endeavor, there are many people whom I would like to thank for bringing this book together.

Thank you to Nicole Tuggle and Carol Taylor for giving me the opportunity to share my knowledge, and a special thanks to my editor, Joanne O'Sullivan, and photographer, Evan Bracken. It was really great working with talented people such as yourselves. And to everyone at Lark Books who had a hand in making this book a success, thank you.

A very special thanks to Susan Bradley for all her help and support in getting me started in candlemaking. You have been a true inspiration and a great friend. I would also like to thank my computer guru, Richard Henry, for your continued support with all my computer endeavors.

Thank you to my family for your support and encouragement through my whole candlemaking career. And finally, my most loving thanks to my husband for his continued support in all of my endeavors.

Index

Resources

Usually, the supplies you need for making projects in Lark books can be found at your local craft supply store, discount store, home improvement center, or retail shop relevant to the topic of the book. Occasionally, however, you may need to buy materials or tools from specialty suppliers. In order to provide you with he most up-to-date information, we have created suppliers listings on our Web site, which we update regularly. Visit us at WWW.LARKBOOKS.COM, click on "Craft Supply Sources," and then click on the relevant topic. You will find numerous companies listed with their web addresses and/or mailing address and phone number.

Dana Brooks is a candlemaker and owner of WWW.FLICKERINGFLAMES.COM, where you can find her made-to-order custom candles, including wedding candles, which have been featured at weddings around the world. She enjoys teaching others this rewarding craft and has numerous successful students. Her web-site offers an extensive line of candles and supplies as well as information relating to candle carving lessons and helpful tips.